GOAL SETTING

MOVE FORWARD
GET OUT OF YOUR OWN WAY

By
Tom Matzelle

Goal Setting
Move forward. Get out of your own way.

Published by Iron Twine Press

www.irontwinepress.com

Book design by Nanette Davis, Qivu Graphics, Woodinville, WA

Printed in the United States of America.

ISBN 978-0-9970600-6-5

10 9 8 7 6 5 4 3 2 1

TABLE OF CONTENTS

CHAPTER ONE

DISCOVERING A DESIRE TO SET GOALS

"You cannot change your destination overnight, but you can change your direction overnight."

— Jim Rohn

If procrastination, following through or seeking support has been a challenge for you I congratulate you for making it to and through this first sentence. What you are about to read covers the habits, the challenges, the creation and the execution of goal setting and getting out of your own way. Anything you find useful or insightful please take and utilize. For the rest, please take it with a grain of salt; if it doesn't fit, don't keep it, though I do hope it makes you think.

This book is not an epic novel, nor does it contain as many pages as War and Peace (thank goodness). What I want to do is keep it simple, provide a few proven processes that have worked for myself and explain a few techniques with a story or two along the way. Then I want you to go out and discover what is possible when you set and follow a plan for accomplishing your own goals.

We all have our experiences that shape us, and memories that we treasure. We also have experiences and memories we'd rather forget. Just after graduating college I moved to Sun Valley, Idaho to enjoy the great weather and landscape, to learn how to ski and to just have fun… while working two jobs to pay for it all. I didn't have much of a plan beyond that. During that time my parents, who had four children and had been married for 32 years, decided to divorce. Maybe because I was the youngest, maybe because I was the only one in my family not married at the time or maybe because I couldn't understand this from a more mature perspective, but the news hit me differently than it did my brother and sisters. It was inconceivable for me to think of my family in two different households; it was difficult to have my image of our family altered.

Anyone who has gone through a loss, a change or a rough patch knows it takes time to work through things and get to a better, healthier spot with these adjustments. Once I had the knowledge of my parents' divorce I was offered great support, but I

2

rejected it. I closed myself off. I disconnected from friends and family members. When asked what was going on, I muttered—"just stuff." I was frustrated, hurt and a little lost. I disclose this to be honest and to show you vulnerability, not for pity. Millions and millions of families go through divorce all the time and have circumstances much, much worse than mine. I share this with you because this unsettling incident is what started me on a journey to my own realizations, which made me who I am today.

Out of those difficult times I discovered a desire to set goals!

After a year of being a distant and unpleasant soul, I decided enough was enough. I wrote a short story and got my feelings and emotions out (very therapeutic) and then I asked myself: *What have I missed out on in the last year while I've had my head in the sand?* At that moment a flood of thoughts and ideas overwhelmed me so I got out a piece of paper and started jotting them all down. I listed any fun events or good times I thought I might have missed over the preceding year. I expanded my list to include goals I wanted to accomplish in the New Year. I wanted to pursue some goals alone, and also achieve other goals with friends and family.

Some of the goals were very trivial and some were very ambitious. After writing down and identifying 83 goals, I stalled. Stalled is the key word because I felt I needed to do more. This was back in January of 1996. I then came up with the idea of going for 96 goals to match the year: 96 goals in 1996. This helped me frame my pursuit and motivated me to finish the list. A week later I had identified 96 goals that I wanted to accomplish by the end of the year.

With the list to guide me, I started off fast and often tackled a few goals together in one day, and several on the weekend. Many of my goals were fun-filled adventures. Some of them were simple tasks like cleaning out my closets, or writing my Nana once a month. Others were much more time-consuming, like going to Germany for Oktoberfest. Well, after a great year of positive behavior and re-energization I accomplished about 78% of my goals. At first glance, maybe that looks like a failure, and I'll admit that thought crossed my mind.

However, as I reflect back, the previous year *I was an unhappy, sad sack that did nothing and then in the New Year I actually rediscovered myself!* Sure, I didn't achieve everything, but I did a lot more than I normally would have done. And I owed it all to the lists, the written goals, that gave me focus and motivation to take on a more constructive and positive demeanor.

As 1996 was ending and the next year was rolling around the corner, I decided to do it again. The goals that I did not accomplish in my first attempt, I rolled over to the New Year. With one year under my belt I decided to take the same approach; I wanted to identify 97 goals since it was 1997. Once again, at first I was coming up with some great new thoughts and ideas, but somewhere around the mid-50s I hit a wall. I was struggling to come up with other fun, challenging and interesting events and experiences. Then I decided to email about 30 of my friends and family for suggestions. I explained to them what I was doing and how I needed some assistance to come up with more fun and interesting goals for the year. The response was overwhelming: a flood of emails and ideas. I finished putting together my list of 97 goals. Some of the ideas were great and some were a little scary—one person suggested skydiving, ignoring the fact that I am not a huge fan of heights. Some of the other ideas were to go camping, white water rafting, horseback riding, to get a straight shave from an old-school barber, bike certain trails and throw a dinner party.

5

1997 seemed to fly by with all these new adventures and great events that brought me both joy and growth. As the year came to a close I had accomplished 82% of my goals, but that still left me with 17 unreached goals for the year. Now, I am a competitor. I'm not sure if that comes from being the youngest or from being part of a very outgoing and athletic family, but knowing I did not reach the entire list for the second year in a row, I decided to create and pursue 98 goals for 1998. I wrote out a few new goals that had come to mind over the course of the past year and then carried over the 17 goals that I did not reach in 1997. I once again reached out to my friends and family to top off my list for the next year.

What I got back this time was even more astounding then the previous year. I was amazed by all the great ideas that were shared with me, but this year I had people writing back saying they loved the idea I had of setting goals and they were motivated to start lists of their own. I also had people reach out to me after reviewing my list and say they would love to take part and do certain goals with me. That was unbelievably exciting and motivated me to move forward. I was doing things I loved and wanted to accomplish and now I had friends and family that wanted to be part of it. It was the ultimate satisfaction to have people not only supporting me, but also wanting to be involved! It changed my life. I had an impact on others. I felt I had gone from pushing people away to now drawing them to me.

The rest, as they say, is history. From then on I kept making a yearly list, altering it over time by the number of goals or the different categories — focusing on family, friends, travel, career, finances, health, etc. Looking back almost 20 years now at the places I have traveled, the adventures I have taken, the things I have learned and the moments I have shared, I truly feel blessed. Sure, there are still a few things that elude me (I have not yet climbed Mount Kilimanjaro or run the New York City Marathon), but I still have time to reach those goals and live those dreams... and I will!

I want my experience to be everyone's experience and that's why I wrote this book. I want to lay out some basic thoughts to get people to start thinking and taking action and hopefully striving to become the best version of themselves as possible. You already have to wake up each day, so why not wake up each day and aim for the things that excite you and give you a bounce in your step?

If you are stuck in a rut, if you want to improve your people skills or if you want to have a sense of progression and achievement, you need to focus. You need to act with intention and give yourself reasons to get up, get out and get moving each day. That's what setting goals is all about: Defining what really matters to you, committing to those things, and then pursuing them until you accomplish them. That's what I did and I'm a much happier person for having done so. That's what I want to help you do and that's what this book is about, so let's move!

CHAPTER TWO

LIFE IS A GAME

"Our greatest weakness lies in giving up. The most common way to succeed is always try one more time."

— Thomas A. Edison

Did you set an alarm clock to get out of bed when you were five years old? No, you probably jumped out and took on the world with a big smile and eyes wide open. Whatever happened, whether you succeeded or not, you woke up the next day and went after it again with enthusiasm and honest effort. What about at ten years old? Fifteen? What about thirty? Forty? At what point do so many of us lose our enthusiasm, passion, and excitement to take on the day and enjoy life with exuberance? At what age did you stop dreaming and start settling for less?

I'll let you in on a little secret: life's just a game. Don't take yourself too seriously, enjoy the journey. In many ways life is similar to baseball. You take a few swings and maybe you get a hit or maybe you strike out, but if you're smart and perceptive you think about what worked and what didn't and learn from it. In a baseball game after you get a hit (or not), eight of your teammates get a chance to bat, then you get another opportunity to apply what you've learned and bat again. In life, as in baseball, very seldom is your current opportunity your last. You'll get another chance even if you whiff at your first attempt.

Many Baseball Hall of Famers excelled by only getting three hits out of every 10 at bat. A .300 batting average (a 30% success rate) makes you one of the all-time best. No baseball player expects to hit a homerun every at bat, and in life you shouldn't expect to either. You don't need to. When you strike out, pop out or just hit a dribbler to first, remember: not even Hall of Famers go 10 for 10. If you learn from those times when you come up short—strike out, fall down and skin your knee, lose the job or just get yourself into a rut—then no at bat is a failure. If you learn from not meeting a specific life goal, then you stand a better chance to meet or exceed your goal during your next turn.

Everyone has those days where everything is going right, your clothes are fitting well, your hair is combed exactly how you want it and you have a little extra bounce in your step! I love those days, but we also know those kind of days are not daily occurrences. Most of us need to work at consistently achieving that extra bounce. It doesn't just come to us naturally. Success, just like failure, is a habit. You can pick up any kind of habit, good or bad. A habit, in time, becomes a behavior, a disposition, an attitude, a characteristic... those traits become YOU and how you see things and—truth be told—how others see you too.

Even how you *think* about setbacks can become a habit, then over time an attitude, and then **eventually you.** Recently I was having a conversation with my friend Jordan who filled me in on the fact he'd just lost his job. It's never fun to lose your job, but for Jordan it was even worse because he and his wife had just adopted twins. So there he sat with a mortgage, a wife counting on him, three young children and no job. Jordan is standing on the threshold of a choice. How will he react to this moment? Where many people would fall into a negative outlook, he can, instead, choose to see this as an opportunity to get a better job, possibly better benefits for his growing family and a more fitting career. His life, like an empty canvas, is his to color. Yes, there will be some uncomfortable moments between now and when he lands steady employment, but this is not the defining moment of who he is or who he will be. It's an opportunity to write the next chapter of his life and he can choose how he wants it to read depending on his attitude, desire and energy level.

Jordan has it in him to achieve whatever he wants to achieve if his attitude is right. He still has his health, he still has his family, and he still has a lot he can be grateful for and a lot he can apply to his new situation. We all do. We need to give ourselves credit for what we're capable of and embrace our greatness. Inventors create out of necessity every day; you can too. You just have to be unabashed about embracing your strengths and sharing them with the world.

But I'll let you in on another secret: the most successful people I've ever met, no matter their age, are the ones who are able to be vulnerable and ask for assistance when they need it. They also know their present circumstances don't define who they are. Jennifer is a friend of mine who runs a nationally successful business distributing books. She wasn't always in the book distribution business. In fact, 10 years ago she was a pharmaceutical rep when she got laid off. She was as devastated then as Jordan is now. She immediately set out trying to land a new position. As she organized herself around that goal, the thought occurred to her that there were probably lots of people in the same boat as her so she decided that as she looked for a job she would also research and write about her experiences and document lessons learned in what it took to successfully land the ideal job. In the end, she decided not to go back to pharmaceutical sales, she was too interested in the idea of sharing what she had learned about the art of the job search. The endeavor turned into a book.

Then it was time to publish the book and sell it. She didn't know the first thing about how to do that. So she did something many of us don't want to do: she openly admitted she didn't know and sought out people who did know for guidance (even though it initially made her uncomfortable to request help). Sell the book to college students who want to find jobs, they told her. *Sell the book to the parents of college students who want their children to find jobs and not move back home,* they said. That's what she did, very successfully, I might add. Now 10 years later she travels the country teaching others how to write, publish and sell their own books. She employs a team of educators who help her share her message and a team of salespeople who help her sell and distribute the four other books she has written since.

Faced with an unsettling setback in her career, Jennifer chose to see it as an opportunity and convert a possible negative circumstance into a positive one.

On occasion you may have encountered someone you didn't like because he or she always got what they wanted; success came easy for him or her. Back in my college days, I hated these types of people. Okay, I really did not hate them, I was just jealous. "Why them and not me?" Then one day I asked myself, "Why can't that be me? Who says that can't be me?" After moments like those, I would often daydream, as I'm sure a lot of us do. My daydreams usually consisted of being the most valuable player on the winning side in whatever sport, or dating the most popular girl at school. Guess what happened?

*In real life, I never became that stud athlete and I never got the girl. Why? Because all I did was dream about it. I didn't understand then what it took to make those **dreams** a **reality.***

You turn your **dreams** into **reality** by first turning your dreams into **actions** — just as I counseled Jordan to do and just as Jennifer did. With a plan, a process, and a consistent effort toward execution you will get where you want to go. It won't happen instantly—it took Jennifer three years to have success in selling her book and ten years to get to where she is now—but if you don't give up and you stay focused on what you want and clear on why you want it, and have no doubt what you are willing to do to achieve it, it will happen.

That is what this book is all about.

Life is about choices—choices we make. Life does not just happen to us. We choose our way through every single day of our lives. We choose to accept a situation or not. We choose to learn from our experiences or not. We choose to set our own direction or to follow someone else's. It's our own choice how we react to our circumstances and how we move forward. It's our own choice to feel sad, mad, happy or motivated.

No one can make you sad unless you let them. That's not to say that sad things don't happen in life. They do. Sadness is an important human emotion and a natural reaction to disappointment and loss. However, sadness should be a transitory state and not a state you live in forever. You can't change the events of your past, but you can choose how you react to those events going forward. If sad things have happened to you, you can choose to let them overwhelm you or you can choose to remain positive and optimistic and move forward. And if you need help to work through some of your past challenges, shortcomings or losses, all you need to do is be honest, (yes, at times even vulnerable) and open to accepting support. With assistance you will hopefully get to the next chapter in your life by putting the last chapter where it belongs… in the past!

CHAPTER THREE

SETTING THE RIGHT GOALS FOR YOU

"The mind is everything. What you think is what you become."

— Buddha

Remember – life is a game. No one is keeping score, except maybe you, so relax. When people relax and enjoy themselves, they are more open to possibilities and opportunities. Make the best of the hard times and cherish the good times. Life is about choices; you can choose to be happy and extroverted or sad and introverted. Choose wisely!

One sure fire way to be more positive and optimistic is by going after your dreams, accomplishing your goals and never letting others stop you. Dedicating your time and energy to the relentless pursuit of your goals, even under the most difficult circumstances, and even when it seems overwhelming, are your choices and that can have a tremendous uplifting effect on your outlook.

Not everybody actively sets goals. A lot of people watch life happen to them without looking to improve or change anything, and then wonder why they aren't getting what they want... they might even blame and play the victim at times.

Why? The five most common reasons people don't set goals are:

1. People don't know how to set goals.

2. People are searching for the perfect way to set goals.

3. People are afraid to set goals.

4. People are afraid to succeed.

5. People are afraid they won't succeed.

Do any or all of these reasons sound like you? If so, you are not alone. You may be afraid to set goals or unsure of how to go about it. The possibility of failure paralyzes you. You can only accept a successful outcome. You hate to lose. To a certain point this is commendable. However, don't be afraid.

I'll make sure I address these five points by the end of this chapter, but the first thing I want to do is just get you in the right mindset around goal setting, so I want to address the first two facts in depth here:

1. People don't know how to set goals.

2. People are searching for the perfect way to set goals.

Before you worry about doing things right, worry about doing the right things.

If you find yourself plagued with fears, perfectionism or doubt while pursuing your goals it may be that you are pursuing goals that are not the right goals for you. It's very easy to let other people tell you what your goals should be. However, it can be very difficult to find the energy and passion to work on goals that have been imposed on you by someone else. Sometimes you kid yourself into believing that a goal imposed on you by someone else is really a goal set by yourself. In reality, all you are trying to do is appease others. Failure is likely in situations like these.

So first things first:

make sure the goals you set are the right goals for you and not goals set by or for others.

There's a simple way to do this. At the beginning, when you define a goal, don't focus on what the goal is, focus on why you are setting that goal. Most people look at what they are going to do, but if you focus on why you are going to do it, you will make choices that are more aligned with who you are and what you want out of your time. Focusing on why gets you to the core of your energy, your passion and integrity.

For example, you have a goal to be more socially active. That's the what and it's a good goal to have. Let's imagine it's a cold, dark, rainy winter night. You had a long, slow commute home. You had planned to go out to a new Meetup group, but by the time you finally reach home you are too tired, cold, and grumpy to even consider going back out again. You say to yourself, "What's the point? No one is expecting me." Your what question should be replaced with a why question such as: "Why should I?"

Because if you do go out, you have the chance to establish new relationships and that has the potential to lead to great things.

"You miss 100% of the shots you don't take."

— Wayne Gretzky

If you did crank up the energy to get out there and follow through on your Meetup plans, you may make connections with other people. Those connections could turn into friendships and those friendships could turn into professional or social opportunities. That is the why question. What you want to be is socially active. Why? Because you want access to opportunities.

Now you're motivated. Now your intentions are clear.

If you know **why** you're pursuing a goal, that will clarify your thinking and intentions, and having that kind of focus will help you access the energy and passion you'll need to succeed.

What you energize lives, what you feed grows, and what you starve dies.

We've talked about why people don't set goals and I hope in the process I have inspired you to overcome your personal goal-setting roadblocks. You're on your way now to being unafraid to set goals.

Which Goals Should I Set?

Think about the quote above: What you energize lives, what you feed grows and what you starve dies. If you want to be an athlete, you need to spend time and energy working out and practicing. If your goal is to get good grades, you need to hit the books and learn. If you want to start a profitable business, you need to understand the basics, have a strong business foundation and platform, and, finally, focus on the three P's – People, Process and Product.

When people set goals they are often overambitious with lofty aspirations, for example, "I will lose 50 lbs. in less than six weeks."

It's difficult to see progress when you have set yourself up with a single large goal without smaller checkpoints to make sure you're on the right path. Lack of progress, or pressure to meet an artificial deadline will kill your motivation. Goals should be small stepping stones on the path to a successful conclusion. Instead of focusing on the end state—lose 50 lbs. in six weeks—you should consider setting goals around the steps necessary to reach that end state. "I will walk 15 minutes a day." Once you're consistently hitting that goal, the next step is "I will walk 30 minutes a day." And so on.

The point is, your desire is the why, the reason you want to set any goals at all. Get clear on why you want to set a goal. Then build a pathway of what (what you're going to do) to get you to what you desire. Start small and manageable; success breeds confidence and confidence gets things done.

EXERCISE

I have a few questions to get you thinking. Write down your thoughts in response to them and be 100% honest (by the way, vulnerability to the truth is a good thing). No one is judging you. Write it on a separate piece of paper and shred it when you're done if you are too fearful to show others right now.

Just be honest.

What do you really want (be very clear)?

Why do you want it (why is it important to you)?

Why don't you have it right now? What has stopped you?

If you answer these questions honestly, you will have completed the first step necessary to blazing the path forward.

Now let's go back to the first five issues from the beginning of this chapter:

1. **People don't know how to set goals** -- Be clear where you are today. Be clear on what success looks like if you meet a specific goal. Have many checkpoints along the way to build on your confidence and to make sure you are on the right path to the main goal.

2. **People are searching for the perfect way to set goals** -- Make sure the goal is important to you and start with the why before the what.

3. **People are afraid to set goals** -- People want to play safe and not take chances. They want to avoid being vulnerable and exposing themselves to a possible failure. It's easy to let yourself off the hook if you haven't committed to anything.

4. **People are afraid to succeed** -- People are afraid of success if they've never succeeded; people are afraid of what they don't know. People stick to what they're comfortable with

and end up limiting themselves. Setting goals and accomplishing them takes work and some people are afraid that success will be too much work.

5. **People are afraid they won't succeed --** Some people are afraid of dedicating all their time and energy in pursuit of a goal without being assured they will reach it. Failure, like success, has valuable lessons to teach you. You should not be afraid of succeeding. And if you fall short of your, see that challenge as a learning opportunity and never give up. Just focus, be clear, learn from your past and do not be afraid to ask for support or direction from others if this move will help you reach your goal. Remember, being vulnerable is a huge asset in life and in changing how you see things and how others see you.

BUILDING POSITIVE HABITS AND BEHAVIORS

Some people seem to always default to constructive behaviors and they are more successful because of it. Others default to lazy or destructive behaviors and they are more likely to fall short of their dreams.

But good news! If you admire the people whose default move is constructive, you can program yourself to be one of them. Here's how.

What's the behavior you'd like to default to? Getting up earlier in the morning? Eating healthier? Exercising more? Whatever it is, commit to doing it every day for 26 days in a row. That is what it takes to get the new behavior embedded into your subconscious and establish it as your new default.

After the 26 days in a row working on that new habit, that goal will go from what you are doing to why you are doing it. Example – walking every day. At first glance you are walking every day for 26 days in a row to a set a pattern and get into a routine. After 26 days in a row you don't force yourself to walk

27

because now you are a WALKER and that routine has been set into a pattern and behavior. It's in your DNA now, it's who you are. Now you have a mindset to walk daily, as you reprogrammed your body and mind to believe that if you don't walk you will feel weird, even guilty, breaking your program because you've built a positive behavior.

The key is taking an activity and forming a habit and routine. In time that habit becomes a behavior and in time that behavior becomes an attitude.

Be careful. It's easy to skip a day or days and if you do your new behavior will not get embedded. You'll have to start all over. Commit to it. Commit to not skipping. Commit to every single day for 26 days in a row. You won't be the same person when it's over.

One other key thing to remember as you embark on putting pencil to paper, sneakers to pavement, energy into motion, is to not mistake activity with achievement. Understand the journey and be clear about what success looks like to you if you reach your goal. You are searching for achievement of your goal, not just activity with no results. Make sure your activities are bringing you closer to your ultimate goal, and that your time and energy is moving the needle in the right direction!

CHAPTER FOUR

WHAT DO YOU REALLY WANT?

"You'll never get what you truly deserve if you remain attached to what you're supposed to let go of."

— Kush and Wizdom

We are working toward the point where you will be able to set very specific goals and utilize skills to achieve them. But let's remain broad for now and keep it simple.

Let's go back to the first question of the previous exercise: What do you really want? Is that question too general or intimidating? Often when I ask clients that question they hesitate and finally say, "I don't know what I want, but I do know what I don't want!"

Okay, let's start there.

Let's choose an example most of us can relate to.

Imagine you're looking for a new job. There are going to be things you desire with the new job opportunity and there are also going to be things you may not want, as well as things that matter to you and things that don't matter as much.

Practice this. Think about your ideal job. What are some things you clearly do not want—for example, *I do not want to be micromanaged, I do not want to travel or I do not want to give presentations to groups.* Got the concept? Okay, now you do it. Write down three things you do not want in your ideal job or career.

EXERCISE

I don't want_____!

I don't want_____!

I don't want_____!

Let's try one more example: dating. If you're looking to get into a relationship, what are some things you would like in a relationship? Don't know? Well, let's think about a few things you *don't* want—for example, *I don't want to date a smoker, I don't want to have a long-distance relationship, or I don't want to date anyone more than five years different in age than myself.*

The reason we're going through this is so you *don't settle for less.* You can find lots of jobs you'll be qualified for, but if it has conflicting aspects that you really don't like, you won't be happy. Same thing applies with a relationship: don't get involved with someone because he or she fell into your lap, or you didn't have to work for it. Get involved because it matches what really matters to you. Instead of settling for less at work, in relationships or in anything else, you have to clearly define your intentions so that you don't end up with "what you can get" instead of "what you really want."

Let's build on what you've done so far. You listed what you do not want; now let's approach it from a positive angle by listing three things you do want. Think of your job again. For example, *I want extensive health benefit coverage, I want a flexible schedule, or I want to work for a global company that is a leader in their field. Also consider the dating or relationship example, what you do want: I want someone with similar values as mine, I want someone who is health-conscious or I want to date someone who is financially self-sufficient and independent.*

This is a process you can apply to any decision you're making regardless of its complexity. I started using this process when I was looking for my first job out of college. My mom helped me define this approach. The primary objective was gaining clarity. She told me to think about the job I was hoping to find and then simply write a list of what I would like and what I would not like in a job. I used a template similar to this:

EXERCISE

Like	Dislike
1.	1.
2.	2.
3.	3.
4.	4.
5.	5.
6.	6.
7.	7.
8.	8.
9.	9.
10.	10.

Pretty simple, right? As an exercise, fill in your likes and/or dislikes when trying to set a goal for yourself. It's a great way to start. It helps filter out all the noise and identify your true intentions. You can then look not at WHAT you can do or are qualified for, but focus on WHY you want to do something.

The idea here is to become accustomed to the habit of focusing on what matters to you. I know this might look overly simple, but you'd be surprised at how many people never take even that simple step of declaring, in writing, what is really important to them. Studies have shown, in fact, that those who write their goals or intentions down are 80% more likely to achieve them than people who don't. You have to commit to someone and something. Writing your lists is you committing to yourself.

Look at the lists you just made. Did anything surprise you in either column?

It's very common to make lists based on the perceptions of other instead of what really matters to you and what you really want. Maybe you imagine someone looking over your shoulder, or you get worried that what you want is not acceptable to others, and you might feel very vulnerable by putting some of your thoughts down on paper, or on your iPad or PC, as your voice is now becoming real. Here's the key: you don't need to share this list with others until you're ready, if ever. This list is for you. So focus on what feels right to you right now. Just remember: your goals might/can change through time.

Everyone has their own definition of joy and happiness, the right way of doing things and what goals should look like. You must find your own definitions.

I can't tell you what's right or wrong. I can only get you to think and assist you in taking action:

- Are you getting what you want out of life?

- Do you know what you want out of life?

- Do you know how to achieve it?

Your priorities will change over time and so may your goals. Just try to remember that life is a game and in a game you get do-overs, timeouts and extensions. Enjoy it and take the pressure off yourself. My only hope is you keep moving and never settle. I can't say in which direction—up, down, sideways or around something—keep moving towards the things that make you happy and fulfilled. Keep thinking about what makes you happy, and why it really matters to you. Once you identify what matters, pursue it with commitment. Very seldom are you fortunate enough to accomplish a goal by doing nothing. You must keep moving towards your objective. You must chase down your wants.

Remember the shark: If it does not keep moving it will die. If you don't like the shark analogy, a very smart man once said it this way: Life is like riding a bicycle, to keep your balance you must keep moving. His name was Albert Einstein.

CHAPTER FIVE

HOW DO I SET GOALS?

"Trust yourself. Create the kind of self that you will be happy to live with all your life. Make the most of yourself by fanning the tiny, inner sparks of possibility into flames of achievement."

— Golda Meir.

If you never practice the small stuff, which are the steps necessary for goal creation, chances are you will not be able to refine your own understanding of what and why something is important to you. The small stuff in creating a goal will help you take measurement of the critical accomplishments in your life.

It's simple, really: if you don't turn your **goals** into **intentions**, then you have to rely on luck. Maybe you'll get lucky and the things you want most will just happen to you. But guess what, that's not likely and you know it.

So what do you do? Well, you set intentional goals.

In Chapter 3, I said there were five reasons *people don't set goals* and reason number one was people don't know how to set goals. I want to go back to that point and give you additional guidelines for effective goal setting. These guidelines will further help you to set effective and achievable goals. *Achievable goals* — that is an important distinction. As you read over these tips, use what works for you and I will also offer other processes and systems later in the book that may be helpful. For now, just try this approach and see how it feels.

State each goal as a positive statement – Express your goals positively. As an example, "I will execute this technique well" is a much better goal than "Don't make this stupid mistake." You're much more likely to succeed if you shift the focus from your fears or things you do not want to do—making a stupid mistake—to actions that will help you achieve success. Similarly, you're more apt to succeed if you focus your energy on actions you will take, rather than those that you won't. For example, "I will eat salad every Monday for dinner" instead of "I won't eat pizza."

Be precise – Set precise goals, putting in dates, times, distances and amounts as needed. "I will walk 15 minutes every night after work" instead of "I will walk more." When you state your goals with a precise and specific language, you can measure progress. When you're able to measure progress, you'll know exactly when you have achieved the goal, and attain complete satisfaction and closure.

Set priorities – When you have several goals, give each a priority. This helps you avoid being overwhelmed by having too many goals, and helps direct your attention to the most important ones. It's key to have a plan, but also critical to have a process. By setting priorities, this helps define your process by guiding you to what you should address first.

Write goals down – You'll remember this from Chapter 4. Writing your goals down crystallizes them and gives them more force. If they're on paper, they're more real. You can even go a step further once you've written them down by taping that paper up in your office, on your bedroom wall or saving the list as your screensaver so you are reminded of your goals all the time. This help you harness and focus the energy you'll need to succeed. I used to carry my list of goals in a planner so every time I would open the planner I would see my list (yes, I know I'm old, but I'm hoping a number of you reading this will be able to relate). After a while I'd get so tired of seeing my list I'd push myself to achieve everything so I could finally get rid of it. By seeing it every day, the list was more on my mind, even subconsciously, than it would be if I didn't have it written down.

Keep operational goals small – I mentioned this to you earlier: if you want to lose 50 pounds don't set that as your goal. That's too big and it's too hard to measure progress. Instead, figure out the operational steps necessary to achieve the weight loss (such as walking 15 minutes a day, lifting weights for 30 minutes three times a week, and eating salad for dinner on Mondays) and set your goals accordingly. Keeping goals small and incremental provides more opportunities for success and reward.

Set performance goals, not outcome goals – You should set goals that you have the utmost control over. It can be quite disheartening to fail to achieve a personal goal for reasons beyond your control! In business, you could set financial goals only to be tripped up by a bad economy or an unexpected change in government policy. In sports poor judging, bad weather, injuries to teammates, or just plain bad luck could be your undoing. If you base your goals on personal performance, then you can keep control of your goals, and draw satisfaction from them.

Set realistic goals – This is a difficult one, because you should reach for the stars, you should stretch yourself to go farther than you've gone before and you shouldn't enter the act of goal setting thinking about limitations first. However, you do have to give yourself a chance to be successful. Failure is disheartening. Success is motivating. I'm 6'5" and I love horse racing. Sometimes I have dreamt of being a champion jockey. Should I set that as a goal for myself? No, not if I'm being realistic. I haven't seen many competitive jockeys over 6 foot or over 200 pounds.

I have a client who wants to be a millionaire in three to five months. Is that a goal she should set? Sure, it's a worthy goal, but she needs to take into account that she is currently $53,000 in debt. Perhaps a three to five month time frame is not realistic.

When you're setting goals, you have to take your current conditions into account and factor those into your plans. In other words, I can't be a champion jockey because the conditions of my physical frame don't support that goal, but I could set a goal to ride a horse in a race. My client probably will not become a millionaire within five months, because the conditions of her current financial position don't support that goal, but she could become a millionaire within three to five years with proper action, clarity, planning and process. Set the goals you want to set, but know the obstacles you face and what you can do and will do to overcome them.

 ## THE POWER OF SELF-KNOWLEDGE

You can't really know how to reach your goals until you really know yourself. You have to really understand your strengths, your blind spots, the things that cause you tension and what challenges you. Identify and understand your natural desires and pains. Are you naturally selfish, detail-oriented or a procrastinator, just to name a few possibilities? Study all your victories and learning opportunities; are there similarities, common denominators, patterns? Knowledge is good, but it's when you do something with the knowledge that you make change happen in your life. Knowledge is not Power; *Applied*

Knowledge is Power.

Sometimes gaining knowledge about yourself is difficult. We all have blind spots about ourselves. It can help to get an outside perspective. Ask a few friends, coworkers and family to give you some feedback—positive and constructive—to see how others see you. Finally, something to really help you understand the patterns in your behavior and improve your success with others is to look into behavioral assessments to explain how different behavior types tend to see the world and why (Disc, Myers Briggs and Insights are all good examples of behavioral assessments).

When you understand what makes you happy, what makes you frustrated (and why) you can begin to plan more pleasurable moments and limit your frustrations. Planning is key. Applied knowledge holds the power.

CHAPTER SIX

WHAT ARE YOU... A DOER OR A THINKER?

"The greatest danger for most of us is not that our aim is too high and we miss it, but that it is too low and we reach it."

— Michelangelo

Comfort Zones, we all have them. They are where our known talents and our tolerance for fear intersect. Undoubtedly, you have to follow your talents when determining your goals, but don't be afraid of going outside your comfort zone. It can open up your eyes to a world that you never knew existed. New challenges can be fun and rewarding. You will gain greater confidence in yourself. You will be forced to learn new talents. To accomplish challenging goals that bring about life-changing success, you may first need to learn to get comfortable with being uncomfortable.

Fear

In Chapter 3 I talked about five reasons people do not set goals. Three of those five reasons involve fear. Setting and accomplishing your goals can help you change and grow, but too often fear intervenes and stops you before you even get started. Fear is that distressing emotion aroused by impending danger, or pain. Whether the threat is real or imagined the feeling or condition of being afraid can be paralyzing.

Let's assess further the concept that fear is an emotion aroused by *impending danger or pain.*

Is it accurate to believe that pursuing goals in your professional or personal life will put you at great risk? Perhaps that is true if your goal is to be a world-famous base jumper sneaking onto skyscrapers and leaping off with a tiny parachute, or if your goal is to be an alligator wrestler on YouTube. All kidding aside, most of us have little to fear when it comes to our goals other than maybe a little embarrassment. How much does fear or possible embarrassment act as a deterrent when it comes to pursuing your goals? Should there be any?

Are you afraid that someone else will think less of you because you tried and failed? It is understandable that no one wants to fail or be embarrassed. However, I encourage you to try to view it differently. It's the achievement or the attempt that matters, not the embarrassment. I like to run, but I am not a great runner. I'm slower than many and less graceful than most. Nonetheless, I get great satisfaction out of setting a specific distance as my goal and achieving it. As I run down the road and cars speed past me, I do sometimes think about how I look to the people in the cars as I lumber along: comical, graceless, slow, etc. Fear of embarrassment drives these types of thoughts. This fear is trying to convince me to quit. You have to find a way to eliminate this fear. I often think to myself *those people in the cars may be laughing at me, but let them laugh. What matters is that I am out here doing it, pushing myself and succeeding while they are in their cars doing nothing.*

When critics lack the courage to act, it is easy for them to pass judgment on those who are making an effort. Just remember, they don't have the courage – you do. I don't run to prove anything to other people. I run to prove something to myself, namely that I can reach whatever goal I set, regardless of how I look. What matters is action, achievement and effort.

Completing goals gives me a sense of satisfaction and pride. This satisfaction energizes me to set my next goal and charge ahead. Goals help me become the person I want to be and live the life I envision.

So don't be overwhelmed by fear. Be prepared for it and push on. When fear tries to intervene, ignore it by reminding yourself of the pride and satisfaction you'll feel when you push past that fear and succeed with your goal.

Everyone has fear; that is normal. The only difference between successful people and those who are not is successful people move forward in spite of fear and do not let it stop them.

Overcoming Fear

How do we overcome fear?

Marie is one of my clients. She had a goal of finding a fulfilling, loving, lifelong relationship. However, she had fears surrounding the challenge and so she struggled. Marie gave me permission to share her story with you. These are her own words:

My marriage fell apart when I was in my early forties. Here I was, expecting to be settling into a happy, mature relationship, but instead I had to start over. I was terrified. I was afraid to grow old alone. Deep down I knew I didn't have to. I knew I could find someone and remarry, but the immensity of the challenge was paralyzing.

I hadn't dated anyone in 20 years. I didn't even know how to date anymore so I signed up for a few online dating services. I figured I could at least exchange a few emails with men who possibly shared compatible interests, hoping that there would be a connection. To my surprise, I got emails asking me if I wanted to text.

Is that how people date now? What do you text about?

Profiles only go so far in helping me understand peoples' personalities. Every first date felt like a blind date or a first job interview. I was exhausted, worried and frustrated. I felt like someone had dropped me in the Himalayas with no training and told me to climb Mt. Everest.

49

Marie came to me hoping I could coach her through this challenging time in her life. It was obvious to her that she wasn't getting the results she wanted, but she didn't have a clear idea of how to define a way forward.

Here's what we can learn from Marie's experience. Marie was suffering from a very common fear, the fear of being alone.

There are five common fears that usually undermine peoples' success:

1. **Fear of Failure**

2. **Fear of Success**

3. **Fear of Rejection**

4. **Fear of Mediocrity or Not Being Good Enough**

5. **Fear of Being Alone**

You might struggle with one specific fear or with multiple fears. All fears have two things in common: fear denies you progress in life and fear gives you a false sense of security. *Fear is in your subconscious; it covers your past shortcomings and uncomfortableness with a new activity while trying to give you justifications why you should stay still or not move forward.*

- Are you afraid of failure? You can't fail, if you don't try.

- Are you afraid of all the new challenges that can come with success? Then you don't pursue new challenges.

- Are you afraid of rejection by someone you hoped would embrace you? You can't get rejected if you keep to yourself in your secured, safe little world.

- Are you afraid of being classified as unskilled or mediocre? Then you don't expose yourself for someone else to judge you.

- Are you afraid to get out of a relationship and stand on your own? Do you worry about growing old with no one else in your life? Then you settle for a person or a situation that is not right for you.

And that brings us back to Marie.

The problem Marie was wrestling with is common when trying to overcome any of these fears. She was thinking too far out into the future. She was afraid of failing, afraid of rejection and afraid of being alone. She fell into the trap of thinking she had *one shot to find her soulmate.* She wanted a quick fix that could only have one outcome: a lifelong relationship. She failed to recognize all the interim steps between her current state and her desired state.

I worked with Marie, coaching her through five simple techniques for overcoming fear. Think about these five steps when you come up against your fear. These steps helped Marie regain her sense of control and movement that kept her from getting frustrated.

1. Start small.

Fear comes in many shapes and sizes. Confronting it doesn't have to be a great feat or a grand gesture.

I helped Marie break down her anxieties into smaller, more manageable pieces. Instead of wondering how she could meet her "all that and bag of chips," I encouraged her to simply think about how she could make new friends through work, social events, hobbies and clubs. By focusing on meeting new people, she improved her odds of reaching her goal without the anxiety and pressure of finding her Soulmate. This is a great example of a **Performance Goal.** Marie shifted the focus from her perfect outcome to the short-term action of making friends. Making friends is the first step to her desired outcome. It was also a great practice for her to come out of her shell and become more open to meeting others. I would rather she practice with future friends and work on her social skills than focus on a potential Mr. Right with no practice. You need practice; practice helps you get closer to perfect. There is less pressure because the demand for immediate success dissipates. New friendships could eventually lead, by a natural progression, to meeting her significant other.

No matter how significant your fears may seem, scaling them down to more manageable sizes is essential for you to overcome them. Slowly step out of your comfort zone and begin moving towards your goal. Have you heard of the old riddle: How do you eat an elephant? The answer: One bite at a time. Anything is doable if you make it small enough. Working together and breaking her goals down into more manageable and achievable steps, Marie conquered her Mt. Everest one step at a time.

2. Have faith.

You must have faith.

Even though achieving your goal may not always happen on your preferred timetable, you must deliberately and methodically press ahead. You must intentionally create a course of action in line with your expectations. You must have faith. Your *intentional* actions will lead to success. The key is intentional action.

On occasion, unconscious actions can put you in a position of having to have faith as a random act, but don't rely on it. If you're not doing anything to work toward your goal and you just believe that the solution will land in your lap, you will be disappointed. Luck normally happens when *Opportunity meets Preparation.* If you are taking intentional steps, even small ones, to make yourself ready (preparation), then you can have faith that achievement is not only possible, but probable. You also stand a better chance at having luck on your side.

Marie had gotten into a rut—work, family, money issues, and so on. Life had become stagnant for her. She'd lost touch with what excited her and gave her energy. She then intentionally created an action plan to break from her rut. She joined various meetup groups and clubs and took a couple of classes (photography, cooking). She made friends and became much more confident from a social perspective. Her new self-confident approach with others eventually led her to the relationship she was hoping for.

3. Write it down.

When I started working with Marie one of the first things I had her do was start a journal. Just like writing your goals down, making a list of your fears is a great way to work through them. Marie started with her list of fears and concerns and also jotted down simple notes about making new friends, and her dating experiences. The journal helped her identify patterns in her thought process and behavior. She was also able to identify and learn from her own blind spots. Daily journal entries enhanced her ability to focus on the characteristics of her persona that mattered in pursuit of her goals.

Like Marie, you'll find it useful to write down your fears and assess them accordingly (not only what your fears are, but why you believe you have those fears). These tasks will provide you with a starting point for you to conquer your fears. You should then chart in your journal or notebook your progress in conquering your fears and challenges associated with them.

Writing also gives you tangible evidence that things are evolving, even if at times they don't seem to be.

4. Accept what develops (or doesn't).

The Dalai Lama once said, "If you have fear of some pain or suffering, you should examine whether there is anything you can do about it. If you can, there is no need to worry; if you cannot do anything, then there is also no need to worry."

Marie succeeded by learning what mattered to her, organizing her activities and reviewing her interactions with other people. She discarded those elements that didn't match her expectations and focused on what did. "I had to accept the fact that the first date might not lead to a second and that he might not be the one," Marie said. "I had to accept that I could not force a relationship, nor could I force the timing of true love. I could only control what I could control and I learned to focus on that."

Letting go of our fears allows us to focus more on the present moment and its challenges, and less on the fear itself.

5. Take control where you can.

The previous section tells us not to worry about what we can't control and it also teaches us to focus on what we can control.

Know yourself and your natural strengths. Get to know what works well for you and don't waste your time on what doesn't. Capitalize on your strengths.

Push yourself and surround yourself with greatness. You are responsible for your own life. You can't expect someone else to do it for you. It would be nice if that support came, but don't sit around waiting for it.

To defeat any fear you must be completely willing to disconnect from the negative and accept what develops (or doesn't). Marie had to accept the fact that the first date might not lead to a second and that he might not be her Prince Charming. She had to accept that she couldn't force a relationship or the timing of true love. She had to force herself to participate with people socially to increase her chances of reaching her ultimate goal.

She took charge where she could and her life is better for it. She found a relationship. Is he her Mr. Right? Only time will tell. Marie, today, is more confident and hopeful. The key here is that now, because she understands the importance of realistic goals and knows what matters to her, she is in charge of the outcomes.

CHOICES:
THE ONES WE MAKE,
WE BECOME

Life is a game. Life can be simple. It all depends on you.

"Stop right there, Mr. Matzelle! You have no idea! I am a single parent with three kids and I have two jobs and health issues. Life is not so simple."

Actually, it is. It may appear to be not easy at a specific moment, but life is all about choices and the choices you make will define the simplicity in your life:

- Family can be a choice. Do we want kids? A lot of children or just one? At what age do we want to try for a family?

- Health can be a choice. Will you be a smoker? Do you eat a tremendous amount of processed food? Do you exercise a little, a lot, or not at all?

I know certain things seem out of our control. Some of them are. As the Dalai Lama said, "No need to worry."

People have challenged me plenty of times on this idea that life is simple. "I have cancer," they might say. "That wasn't my choice. What's your smartass answer to that one?" Cancer is scary. Cancer is tough. My nana, mom and sister have all had breast cancer. I understand how it can affect people and their loved ones: pain, disfigurement, frailty, abandonment, debt, and much worse. Cancer, like other calamities, can happen, but until they do they are just fears, just thoughts and emotions wrapped around a possibility.

When you are stricken with cancer, it is the emotional reaction that can cripple you. It is only natural to expect the worst. You must remain positive. I have found that often (not always) those who choose to keep things positive and choose to keep things simple have a higher success rate and a better chance of recovery. I can speak of this firsthand as my mother and sister are long-term cancer survivors. What I've observed is that when people don't let the news of the diagnosis break them, they maintain the strength to move forward without giving up hope.

Belief in hope can give you strength to endure and succeed. Belief in yourself can give you the same strength, and if you're willing to commit to a process and a plan you create your best chance for success. Don't get overwhelmed or intimidated. We are what we think we are. Are you happy, sad, rich, poor, healthy? Do you feel ugly, confident or powerless? Some people will praise, compliment and inspire you and others will malign you. This also applies to how you judge yourself. You should program yourself to appreciate the praises and disregard the destructive criticisms. Talk can be cheap. Imagine how your life could be so much more constructive if you simply chose not to listen to the noise.

EXERCISE

Bear with me. This is an exercise that looks incredibly irrelevant on the surface, but it can have a profound effect on your understanding of how you choose to hold onto things even when they no longer serve you.

If you're in a rut or want to change things up, you should really start at home. Most of us are creatures of habit to a fault at times. If our behavior fails to produce the results we want, then why do we continue behaving the same way? If you want to strive for something better, then you have to learn to clean out your closets—the closet of your habits and expectations. You can start with learning how to clear out your real closet first.

Look in your bedroom closet.

Do you have things in there that are out of style, that don't fit anymore, or that you never wear? Why are they still there? Get rid of them. Rid yourself of shoes, shirts, blouses, and old shrunken torn or faded garments that are just taking up space. Are you one of those who look all put together to most people, but if someone happened to open up one of your closets they would be knocked over by a landslide of the junk or embarrassments that you are trying to conceal?

We tend to wear 20% of our clothes 80% of the time. Donate what you don't wear to Goodwill. Straighten and clean things up and get organized. No throwing stuff in a pile anymore or stashing them in the dark corners of your closet. People who are organized with less baggage tend to be more successful.

When you're done with the closets (bedroom, hallway, and your basement and attic if you want to tackle a larger exercise), clean out your car. Organize your trunk and glove compartment. Then clean out and organize your bathroom. Once you have everything organized to your satisfaction, keep it that way. If it takes too much time to keep things organized daily, touch everything up on the weekends. Make a schedule and hold yourself to it.

As you clear out your things, you will probably ask yourself more than once, "Why am I still hanging onto this?" Once you dispose of it, you will experience a sense of relief and accomplishment as well as feel lighter and more organized.

Often your emotional closet is stuffed with friends, job issues, significant others, domestic challenges, eating habits, personal care needs and so on. How many of these occupiers no longer serve you? How many are not helping you the way you want them to? Why is your emotional closet stuffed with redundancy and non-factors in your life? **You can choose to clear them out too.**

CHAPTER SEVEN

A WASTE OF TIME IS JUST THAT!

"Don't it always seem to go that you don't know what you've got 'til it's gone."

– Joni Mitchell, Big Yellow Taxi

Where does water come from?

If you live in a developed country, you may answer that question as simply as "from the faucet."

Of course that's not true. There are countless water sources. According to Water.org, the average American uses 176 gallons of water per day while the average African only uses 5. Most Americans don't even think about water. Americans just assume there will always be water.

Why am I talking about water? Because I want to make a point about Time. Most of us treat time the same way people in the developed world treat water. We don't think about it. We assume there will always be time to do things. We waste time like we often waste water.

If you know how to set goals, you're off to a good start, but you also need to know how to direct your energy to achieve your goals. Directing your energy to achieve your goals requires that you do two very important things:

1. Recognize that time, like water, is not an endless resource; and

2. Gain control over how and where you use time.

Today is the oldest you've ever been and the youngest you'll ever be again. Make today count!

You can't recycle wasted time. When it comes to planning and setting goals one of the biggest hurdles is wasting time. You have the power to avoid wasting time. Don't be a Time Waster! **Wasting time can be a habit.** Some of us are guiltier than others. It hinders your ability to achieve your ultimate goal in the allotted timeframe and it also contributes to unnecessary stress along the way.

Occasionally time-wasting circumstances are random occurrences and beyond your control, such as bad traffic, a sick child, or a delayed flight. Prepare yourself for unforeseen delays and develop backup strategies to minimize their impact.

Some people are compulsive time wasters. These individuals do not have the strength to seek closure. The lack of action saps the energy out of their existence. It's futile to direct your energy toward achieving your goals if you don't have any energy left.

Time wasters can also show up in the form of other people who either consciously or unconsciously try to influence you. Because of them you give up your ability to avoid fruitless investment of energy, time, money or attention. Time wasters can also be non-productive activities like reading emails, perusing social media, internet surfing or watching TV at home. We've all been there. Eventually you will wonder *how did so much time go by with so little to show for it?*

The truth is that engaging in these types of interactions is an act of free will. We can only blame ourselves for getting sucked in once again. We must walk a fine line between productive time and wasted time. On occasion, it is necessary to relax and to blow off steam. Being unfocused is good for us in short doses, but anything without limits can become a liability.

Combating Time Wasters

Here are a few basic things to consider when addressing the time wasters:

1. **Respect your need for sleep by getting 7 to 9 hours of sleep each day.** Cutting out sleep to have more fun or get more work done is a shortsighted strategy. While you can temporarily pull this off to a degree, it is a destructive habit. Being tired all day means that you will not be able to make effective use of your time, no matter how organized you are. So make a habit of getting those legitimate seven to nine hours each night.

2. **Do a weekly review of the past 7 days.** Learning how to do a weekly review is one of the best time management habits you can develop. The Weekly

Review is a concept created by David Allen, author of the classic productivity book Getting Things Done. First, review your calendar for the past week and the current week. Look for loose ends, meetings and other matters that need further attention, prioritize accordingly and delegate where possible

3. **Focus on a single task at a time (i.e. no multitasking!).** Multitasking is a wasteful way to work. You will achieve more if you choose one activity at a time.

4. **Separate strategic and "brain dead" tasks.** High value strategic tasks are what companies and clients pay for—coming up with new product ideas, ways to reduce cost and other improvements. However, it is difficult to deliver creative insights all day long. There is such a thing as the law of diminishing returns. Once you reach a natural breaking point on your strategic tasks, then take care of the "brain dead" tasks—i.e., unloading the dishwasher, mowing the lawn, or food shopping. Brain dead tasks require your presence, but not as much of your creative abilities.

NOTE: A good project management tool for larger tasks is Work Breakdown Structure (WBS). You can learn more about it at http://www.workbreakdownstructure.com/.

5. **Accomplish large projects by breaking them down into smaller tasks.** The ability to accomplish large projects is one of the most important time management hacks. For example, if you are assigned with organizing a corporate conference in six months, the effort may feel impossible. Get started by writing a deployment task plan, seek advice from people who have accomplished similar projects, and then work on the deployment tasks, one at a time.

6. **Set a number of priority tasks per day to ensure success.** At the beginning of the day, it is easy to come up with a to-do list with dozens of items. Unfortunately, unplanned phone calls, requests from the boss and others quickly overturn the best plans. Instead, simply choose a number of important tasks per day to ensure success. The priority list can be fixed to three a day depending on complexity. In other words, the set number should facilitate success.

7. **Use your values to make decisions about your time.** Understanding yourself is essential to managing your time. For example, if your top value is family then you will have to manage your work requirements according to that value. Are your actions in alignment with your stated values? You say family is your top priority but you work 80 hours a week. There's no right or wrong answer

here, I'm just encouraging you to organize your time so that it supports what is most important to you. Discovering your values is challenging if you have never given thought to this area before.

8. **Admit mistakes quickly and move on.** Pride is a great thing but it can also take down dreams and empires. Covering up mistakes wastes everyone's time, including your own. You can achieve much more in life if you admit to your mistakes, solve the problem and move on. Most people are willing to forgive mistakes, especially if you are honest and work hard at preventing the mistake from occurring again. Mistakes are just learning opportunities; don't be too hard on yourself.

What Is Time Management Anyway?

If you ask a group of people to define "time management," they will probably talk about getting it all done, crossing items off of a list, and being productive. However, the best time management tips do not involve cramming more and more into your day. The most valuable time management tip involves learning to dedicate your time on those activities that are most meaningful to you.

71

Time Management Tip #1:
Be Efficient and Effective

Efficiency means getting a lot done in a short time, but effectiveness happens when you also focus on activities that matter to you. As the old saying goes, you can run as fast as you want, but if you're going in the wrong direction, you won't end up where you intended.

Time Management Tip #2:
Learn Where Your Time Goes

How you know you've been seduced by a time waster is when you find yourself:

- watching TV shows you don't really care about

- checking email over and over throughout the day

- surfing the internet or cruising YouTube with no purpose in mind

- wandering around stores, just looking for bargains

- spending a few hours every day running errands

- shuffling the same papers back and forth on your desk

Time Management Tip #3:
Draw the Line

The good news is that it's easy to change these mindless habits that monopolize your time management. All it takes is a conscious choice to spend your time differently by implementing a little advance planning:

- When you come home, leave the TV off and find a more meaningful way to decompress (go for a walk, read a book, play with your kids). Be more selective with what you watch on TV and record the chosen few shows that you can watch at your leisure without compromising your time.

- Get into a routine of checking email no more than 3 times a day (morning, noon, and evening). Turn off the "you've got mail" alarm.

- If you lose track of time while web-surfing, set a timer to go off in 15 or 20 minutes. Make yourself get up and turn off the computer when it dings.

- For 30 days, shop only from a list. Only go to stores that carry the item you need, and if you don't actually need anything, don't go shopping in the first place.

- Set aside a single "errand day" each week and sit down with your family to plan your list. Put everything you need in one basket by the door, and plot your route in advance to avoid backtracking. If someone forgets an errand, either insist that it wait until the next errand day, or let them do it themselves.

- Take 5 minutes to sort through incoming papers every day. Put "to-do" papers into a tickler/action file, and set aside time once a week to file and handle to-dos. Set up a spot for papers you're currently working on, and take 5 minutes to clear your desk before you leave each day

Time Management Tip #4:
  Make Time for Your Priorities

Try to look for a way to free up hours of time in your schedule each week to help you with pending priorities. Be sure to use the time on your priorities. Block off time in your schedule for "must" projects. Don't allow other less important tasks to disrupt your schedule. If someone asks you to do something else during that time slot, let them know you can't because you already have another appointment (you do – with yourself!) and enjoy the satisfaction you get from being loyal to your time management skills!

These time management tips can help you do more of what you want with your week.

Now don't get me wrong. I am not saying to give up the things that you enjoy on your down time or that recharge you; just be conscious of the amount of time you spend on them. I love TV as much as anyone, but if I planned to watch a football game at 10 a.m. until 1 p.m. and end up watching three games into the evening, then I failed to meet my time management objectives. I would not have been able to complete my other planned tasks, whatever they may be for the day. I would have wasted my time. Don't be tempted; develop a plan you can stick to and then stick to it.

THINK LESS, DO MORE

Do you do this: you make task lists to guide your work from day to day but you never complete all the tasks? Some of the things on the list are fun to do and others you don't look forward to so you skip those things. I'll let you in on an important secret: successful people don't put things off.

Here's my challenge to you: act on your ideas the moment you think of them. Do as much as you can right away and within 24 hours of identifying a task write down a time by which it will be done.

We tend to have energy to complete an idea when it's new because it's exciting. When an idea sits too long without any action taken on it, it becomes stale and it starts to feel like a nuisance, too difficult. Don't let yourself fall into that trap. When you think it, do it.

CHAPTER EIGHT

YOU ARE
WHO YOU HANG WITH
AND WHERE YOU
SPEND YOUR TIME

"You are only going to be as good as the people you surround yourself with. Choose wisely."

— Tom Matzelle (Hey, that's me!)

Two of the biggest influences in our lives are our environment and our relationships. Relationships not only mean interfacing with our work colleagues, friends, and family, but more importantly with ourselves.

Jim Rohn stated that any one of us is the combination of the five people we spend the most time with. Their intelligence, income, health, happiness and their success are similar to who you are. As the saying goes, you can't pick your family, but you can pick who you spend your time with. Whom you pick matters.

Sometimes there are conflicts with who we say we want to be and who we tend to spend most of our time with each day. For example, if you want to get into better shape than you are today, you might want to hang with a group that is into exercising, eating healthy and staying fit. If the group that you spend a lot of your time with is in direct conflict with your getting into shape because they'd rather stay out late, eat unhealthy food and drink a lot of empty calories, then you are less likely to achieve your fitness goals hanging around that group. You simply aren't operating in an environment that supports and encourages your vision. If that's the case, you may want to choose a different group and upgrade your influences.

You must **be** who you **strive to be**, not who you will **settle for**. It's not fair to your friends, family, coworkers or yourself if you choose to settle for being less than you could be.

So how do we figure out who's in your core group of five? Think about the 5 people in your life that you

78

spend the most time with and talk with on a regular basis, not just in one day, but on average over a week or, better yet, a month. How many hours of your day are spent with them? I'm guessing they will be your spouse, other family members, coworkers and close friends. Write those five people's names on a piece of paper. Once you have your list, ask yourself this: What are they passionate about? How ambitious are they? How successful have they been? How happy, optimistic and authentic are they? Be careful not to gauge success with money. Those who have a strong bond with family and friends and a healthy outlook are wealthier in their own way.

Carefully evaluate if the people that you wrote down are the ones that will really help you achieve your goals. Do they challenge, support and assist you to get to the next level, or are they pessimistic, uninterested, helpless and selfish?

If you hang out with successful and positive-minded individuals who believe in accepting the consequences of their actions, you more than likely will become a similar individual. Being in control of and responsible for your actions ensures success in life. If you hang out with a bunch of pessimistic individuals who believe the world is out to get them and there is nothing worthwhile to challenge, you will eventually descend into a downward spiral of negativity.

When I first finished college I was still hanging with a number of my drinking buddies from school. We stayed out late on weekends, burned the candle at both ends and didn't have the best eating habits. Then one day a friend told me about a marathon he was going to run. I thought that sounded interesting and two weeks later I signed up for the race myself. I started training, but I didn't change my habits of staying out late and eating junk. My friend who got me into running my first marathon asked me how things were going a few weeks before the race. I told him it was hard as I was trying to juggle my social life and my eating habits were hardly stellar. He asked me who I spent my time with and how they ran their lives. I guess he was not too impressed as he told me to be successful you need to put yourself in a position to be successful. He told me to come with him three days a week and join his running club. He also introduced me to healthier alternatives and also a few other friends that were runners. Hanging with those new friends made it easier to get in (and stay in) the shape I needed to be in to be successful. After six weeks training with him, I finished my first marathon. I actually did a lot better than I first thought I would and I learned a key lesson: It's easier to be successful when you surround yourself with the right people, tools and resources.

This mindset is especially important in goal achievement, because your consciousness affects the kind of thoughts and actions you undertake. If you want to lose 20 lbs., you need to ensure your mindset/consciousness is disciplined enough to make the difficult choices to stay the course. As previously stated, if you are constantly surrounding yourself with people who eat a lot or binge-eat, you will have a greater difficulty in fighting off temptation. Your ability to stay on track will boil down to how grounded and resilient you are. Think how much easier the task becomes if you are hanging out with likeminded people with similar visions. They will provide moral support and be a positive influence.

How do you surround yourself with individuals who have the same work ethics and perspectives?

Here are a few questions to ask yourself to help you get into a group that is more likeminded and, more importantly, will provide the support you need to achieve your goals. I am NOT saying leave your friends that you have today, but you may want to branch out and make others who are a closer fit to who you want to become. Remember, you are shaped by who you spend your time and energy with.

Here are some questions you should ask yourself:

1. What kind of person do you want to be?

What is your ideal self that you wish to become? What are the qualities you want to possess in relation to your health, finances, friendships, family, and state of mind?

2. Who are the 5 people you spend the most time with in your life currently?

What are they like? What are the top three characteristics they possess? Are those characteristics those you want to emulate?

3. Do they match who you want to become in the future?

Do their qualities match who you want to become? Do they enable or disable your vision of yourself? Do they motivate or hinder you?

4. Who are the top 5 people who embody the qualities you desire?

Are they people you know personally or people you follow? They should be people you aspire to become and/or respect in some way another.

5. How can you befriend them or nurture a beneficial connection?

Do you have compatible qualities or interests to be able to establish some form of a bond professionally or personally?

There are some simple things you can do to connect with the people you respect or admire:

Direct contact:

How can you increase the opportunities of interfacing with someone you may not know today? If you don't know the person, do you have any friends who might know this individual? Does this person belong to any clubs, groups or a community you can be part of? Is there a way for you to participate in the same social circles or to be introduced to them? If you know the individual, how can you communicate with him/her more often? Can you set up a regular face-to-face meeting? How about if you ask them if you could discuss points of interest over the phone once a month? You'll find that people are often much more willing to give their time than you expect them to be. People like to be sought out for sincere reasons if they know you wish to learn and you respect them. Connect or follow them on Twitter, Instagram, Snapchat, LinkedIn and Facebook.

Products of their work:

Establishing direct communications takes planning, effort and time. Sometimes it might not work out, so you may want to indirectly seek out or learn from a person of interest through other means. Does this person publish his works, host seminars or podcasts? Does she have a social media platform? Can you follow him on his blog? You can learn from her indirectly.

I have a friend who is an aspiring chef. One of her favorite chefs had a Twitter account. She followed him. Through time she was able to interact with him by posting questions about recipes and techniques. He responded. She continues to correspond and learn from him via his Twitter account.

Know What You Don't Know:

Regardless of whom you connect with and how you make that connection, you will only benefit from the connection if you are honest with yourself and admit when and where you need help. Asking for help and assistance and admitting you are human is difficult, but it will help you take that next step to get closer to your goal. They say it takes a village to raise a child, no one does it alone. I believe it takes a village, a special support team, to make anything significant happen.

Being open, vulnerable and willing to expose your desires and lack of knowledge may be hard for you. However, expressing that you need some help and guidance will be an important step in becoming who you want to be. No one does it alone. You are wasting your time if you try to do it alone every time. *Work smarter with others and not harder alone.*

Remember, I've said all along that we have choices in life. We can choose where we live and where we work, we can choose to be happy or unhappy, and we can choose to display positivity or negativity. We can also choose who we spend our time with. Answering the above questions will assist you with

85

what you need to do to find the people who embody the qualities you admire.

To quote, Socrates: "I know that I do not know." To be able to admit this is a sign that you are open to guidance and ready to learn and being ready to learn is the first step in success.

In life, as we grow, we go through three stages:

I don't know what I don't know.
I know what I don't know and
I know what I know

It is impossible to quantify how long it may take an individual to become knowledgeable in a concept, technique, process, or perspective. After a short period you may have a general understanding but you still know less than what you don't know. The timeframe of gaining knowledge can be hours or a lifetime. The decision on how much you want to know is an individual choice. Do you want to fiddle with a violin for fun or do you want to be a professional violinist? Do you want to be able to get by with basic Spanish or do you want to master it? The key is that you pursue knowledge. It's just your choice how knowledgeable or capable you want to be at something new. Talent, focus and desire are also part of your pursuit of knowledge. It all depends on how far you want to go, but I can promise you if you don't have a plan, focus and goal along with the energy and proper choices, it is unlikely you will achieve anything.

Remember, having healthy relationships with a teacher, a mentor, a coach, or someone you really look up to and respect can only help you in your pursuit of knowledge. They shorten the distance between START and SUCCESS and save you energy, money and time.

PLUS ONE

If you really want to be successful, then doing just enough is never enough. Your success lies one step past "just enough." So try a Plus One whenever you can.

What's a Plus One? It's pushing yourself to do a little more each day in pursuit of your goals than you did the day before. For example, if you do 50 push-ups a day, your Plus One would be to try for 51. When you achieve that, then shoot for 52. Then Plus One again, 53, and so on. If you run 3 miles, your Plus One could be 4 miles. At work you might turn in a project a day early or stay one hour later to finish it up. You're just taking your effort level and you are extending your goal a bit further than you originally planned by doing a Plus One. If you did a Plus One while reading a book daily and your Plus One was to read an extra chapter each night, in the course of a year you'd have read an extra 365 chapters.

Plus One isn't much, it's just one more. But your little efforts over time become a lot!

CHAPTER NINE

THE MENTAL GAME OF GOAL SETTING

"I'm a slow walker, but I never walk backwards."

— Anonymous

Four key outputs in the successful pursuit of goals are:

Choice:

The right choice will focus your attention and direct your efforts in support of the relevant activities for success. The right choice eliminates the undesirable and irrelevant.

Productivity:

Goals will lead to more productivity because you will be smarter in the way you accomplish your tasks at hand.

Persistence:

Success will make you more persistent in pursuing new goals.

Cognition:

Lessons learned will make you aware of what it takes to develop as an individual and implement positive changes in your behavior.

It's undeniably important to set concise goals to maximize your energy constructively. However, you must believe in your goal or you will not succeed. Remember, you are what you think you are.

On May 6, 1954, Roger Bannister accomplished something that was widely believed to be impossible. He became the first person in recorded history to run a mile in under four minutes. Bannister ran track at Oxford and was a member of the English Olympics team. Despite conventional wisdom at the time, which declared a sub-four-minute mile impossible, Bannister believed differently and saw himself breaking the record someday. On that May day in 1954, in Oxford, England, his belief became a reality. He finished the 1-mile race with a time of 3:59.4. The crowd instantaneously knew what had transpired. The roar of the stadium crowd drowned out the announcer as he stated the record time. The unattainable had finally been attained. Less than a month later, John Landy, an Australian runner, broke Bannister's record and just two months later in a head-to-head competition, Bannister defeated Landy while setting a new record of 3:58.8. Today, the world record time for the 1-mile is 3:43.13.

How can something that was considered impossible first be accomplished by Roger Bannister and then bested time and time again? The mental game of goal setting is the reason. Bannister believed he would beat the 4-minute mark when no one else did. When he broke the mark, that milestone changed the mindset of every other runner in the world. Mentally, they knew it was possible and their physical output changed to match their mental state.

Regardless of what your goal is, you can achieve the same shift in mindset and improve the likelihood of success by learning the practice of **Affirmation**.

ABILITY determines what you are capable of doing. MOTIVATION determines what you do. ATTITUDE determines how well you do it.

There's a saying: "Be the change you wish to see in the world." You hold the power; nothing is cast in stone and it only takes one person to start a movement. For you to be the change you wish to see, you must believe in the change you wish to be.

If you want to change things in your life, you have to believe change is possible. The good news is you can train yourself to believe.

If you want to run a 7-minute mile and are presently running a 7:40 minute mile you need to be in the proper physical shape. Diet, practice, weights, sprints, and long-distance running are imperative. You will never achieve the 7-minute mile if you don't have a desire and a mental outlook that believes it is possible. The same is true if your goal is to pass your SATs or get into the college of your dreams. A way to work on your mental process is through affirmations.

AFFIRMATION is the act of asserting that something exists. Affirmations change the impossible to the possible.

Do you want to be a dynamic and successful public speaker? Then tell yourself "I am a dynamic and successful public speaker" and not "I want to be" or "I hope to be," but "I am." Do you want to be a successful author? Then view yourself as a successful author instead of an aspiring author.

Make your affirmation short, sharp and in the present. Recite it to yourself and not to others. Say it repeatedly, say it every day, say it the same way, convince yourself and become that person. Our heads are too often full of negative voices telling us we can't achieve what we desire. You need to become the positive voice in your own head declaring that you have what it takes. You need to affirm as if you are already experiencing that which you desire.

Is it your goal to be the top salesperson in your company? Then present yourself that way, believe in it and affirm it to yourself: "I am the top salesperson in the company." Be sure to affirm in the present tense. Affirming in the future tense only reinforces subconsciously your doubts about having the ability to be a top salesperson. The future is not real time; the present is. Reality will catch up to your vision if you truly believe.

Your affirmation must be positive. Your affirmations need to excite you. This is you; this is your future! Be direct and confident in the way you phrase your affirmation. Dare to dream big. Don't skimp on your affirmation!

Affirmations are all about getting you in the right frame of mind to pursue your goals. An affirmation is positive thinking. Positive thinking will facilitate success. Here is a checklist you should consider:

Focus on the WHAT, not the HOW. Often we don't pursue our desires because we can't find a logical path to success. Affirmations program your subconscious to bring about your dreams. Don't only go for what you can rationally see yourself achieving today, go for what ultimately excites you.

Affirmations should not be time-sensitive. You are reinforcing what you want to do or want to be and not the time to accomplish it. Deadlines are not the objective. If you don't meet the deadline, you will feel like a failure and be discouraged. Affirmations shape who you are. Affirmations set the goals and the goals establish the timeline. Affirmation is a leap of faith that you can take control of your life and play an active role in creating your own future.

Repeat your affirmations to eliminate skepticism and doubt. Affirmations may at first appear doubtful. You may be skeptical. That is understandable. However, if you repeat your affirmations regularly over time, you will start believing in your affirmations. You will realize that it's counterproductive to think you can't have what you desire. This realization is a sign of constructive progress.

Act on the intuitive signals. Once you begin daily repetitions of your affirmations, you will discover new ideas and thoughts to assist you in pursuit of your desires and goals. It is important you act on these intuitive signals. Often they are creative ideas springing from your unconscious mind. These are signs of additional progress.

Affirm with passion. Until you can feel excited and connected to your affirmation, there is little chance it will manifest itself. Passion creates dominant thoughts. Dominant thoughts have a greater chance of manifesting themselves in your life. Exercise your affirmative passion by embracing the excitement of fulfilling your desires.

Repeat daily. You have countless thoughts every day and many of them can be negative and limiting.

To give your affirmations the best chance of manifesting themselves you need to saturate your mind with them. It is imperative that you say them out loud and with passion regularly: when you wake up, when you go to sleep and when you have a quiet moment during the day. Spend time imagining how your life will look when you have what you desire. Besides thinking it, don't be afraid to write it down several times a day. By saying it you'll absorb it audibly. By writing it you'll absorb it visually and experience it kinesthetically. The more you use your senses in this process, and the more often you repeat it, the more likely you will cement this affirmation in your belief system.

Make affirmation concise. Most people can find many things they'd like to change about their lives. If you are too broad and say you want everything to improve you will weaken the power of affirmations. Try just one or two affirmations to start. Be concise. Focus on one thing you would love or desire in your life. Concision shortens the time to make your affirmation a dominant thought and part of your subconscious. Once you have accomplished this, then it is just a matter of time before your desire becomes a reality.

EXERCISE

Your Turn

In the spaces below, write two affirmations related to your goals. Make one personal and one professional. Remember, make them about who you are in the future, but state them in the present tense. Return to these daily, repeat them, and believe in them.

Personal Affirmation:

I am_____

_____

_____

_____

Professional Affirmation:

I am_____

_____

_____

_____

When I got out of college I realized one of my strengths was my ability to work with other people using my verbal skills. I wanted to use those verbal skills and I wanted to travel. I realized I would love to get paid to be a public speaker and a trainer.

I managed to get a job in the training and facilitation department. That's when my career path began to follow the affirmation I'd always repeated to myself that "I am a public speaker that gets paid to speak." Today, 17 years later, I am a professional Individual and Corporate Coach and I also do public speaking. I've worked with CEOs of Fortune 500 companies, professional athletes, as well as high school and college students and entrepreneurs. All because I knew who and what I wanted to be and I reminded myself of that every day through my affirmations. I can't tell you how long it will take you to reach your personal vision through affirmation, but I promise you if you quit today you will never get there.

OUT OF THE BLUE X 7

A willingness to try new things is a key to success. That's how you find out what you're good at, what you like, and, yes, the things you're not good at and the things you don't like. Look, not everything works out the way you want it to, but you can't let the possibility that something won't work out stop you from doing new things. You have to get used to living outside your routine. Here's an exercise that can help: do something totally out of the blue for seven days in a row. Take a long walk with your wife, buy the coffee for the person behind you in line, volunteer, or try something new on a menu. When you find yourself in a situation where you would normally say "No," just this once say "Yes." As long as it doesn't hurt anybody, just mix things up and see what comes of it. It may frighten you, but you may like it, and you'll never know until you try. I will promise you this: you'll never get to somewhere new doing the same old things. If your goal is to reach something you've never had before, then you must try something new.

CHAPTER TEN

YOU ARE IN CONTROL

"Everybody has their own Mt. Everest they were put on this earth to climb."

— Seth Godin.

In college, my friend Ben almost flunked out in the first year. His grades were terrible—so bad he was summoned to the dean's office and put on academic probation. None of us thought he'd be back after freshman year.

But he did come back and in our second year it was like he was an entirely new person. Any time I wanted to find him, instead of checking the community lounge or looking for at the gym or bar, I just had to go to the library. Any time he had a test coming up, I'd get a little nervous for him, remembering that the year before he'd failed nearly every test. In that first year, if I ever asked him how he thought he was going to do on a test, he'd laugh, sometimes he'd swear at me and he would always shrug like "who knows," like it was a total mystery whether he was going to pass or not. To my surprise at the start of our second year every time I asked him how he was going to do on a test, he had one answer: "I'm going to get an A."

And you know what? He did on every test that year, for every class. And it went on that way the rest of his college career. Upcoming test–"how are you going to do?" – "I'm going to get an A"– A. This kid who failed his way through freshman year and ended up nearly booted out of the university was on the stage at our graduation four years later, at the podium, introduced by the president of the university to speak to all of us as the outstanding graduate in our department.

Ben is a great example of what is possible when you decide what really matters to you and you commit to it 100%. Ben, and the transformation I saw him undergo in college, remains an inspiration to me. He's proof that who you are is not who you must be and that where you are now is not where you must remain—it's just the place you're starting from if you choose to get moving.

Ben is still one of the most positive and successful people I know. He created his own positive outcomes in life because he built an attitude that made any other outcome not just unacceptable, but impossible. That is what I've been showing you in this book: how to achieve the things you want to achieve.

It starts with goals: know where you are today and know where you want to get to. Once you are clear on your goals, take stock of your habits, and the ways you spend your time. Are they supporting or undermining your ability to reach your goals? If you are undermining your own success, change. Determine what behaviors you should have to be successful and then train yourself to perform them, commit to them, and repeat them until they become second nature, and they become your new default. Out of this something amazing and life-altering will happen: your whole attitude toward life will transform. Your attitude is who you are in relation to the world. It grows out of knowing what matters to you. Support your goals by altering your behavior as necessary. Surround yourself with people and allocate your time so that you achieve what is important to you. Stick to your plan and move forward.

I hope you'll try the practices and consider the ideas I've spelled out in this book. What works for you, keep. What you need to alter or add to in order to match who you are or what you want to achieve, do.

Just remember, the choices are yours to make, no one else's. You are in control and the only person who can get in your way and stop you is yourself. If you find that happening, move. Move out of your own way, move forward, just move. Movement will change your life. Phil Knight of Nike says Just Do IT; I say just MOVE and be clear of your why and put yourself in the best position to be successful. Make goals, focus on your intentions, be aware of your time wasters and who you are spending your time with and whether those people are supporting you in your pursuit of your goals.

Life's a game so have fun and just make sure you are playing your game and no one else's! And if you whiff at a pitch or even strike out or skin your knee, learn from your past and make your next opportunity count.

"It always seems impossible until it's done."

— Nelson Mandela

ABOUT THE AUTHOR

Tom Matzelle is an individual and corporate performance coach. His objective is to teach you high-performance strategies and processes allowing you to optimize your time and productivity while bringing out the best version of yourself or business. Born in New York, Tom grew up in Olympia, WA. After getting a BA in Communications, Tom worked for Dale Carnegie and then went on to lead Training and Development divisions for a number of global corporations and Fortune 500 companies including MCI and Expedia. Tom has coached and led courses and spoken to audiences in over 18 countries and such cities as Sydney, Hong Kong, New York, London and Geneva, Switzerland.

"Most people play too small," Tom contends. *"Either because their confidence has been undermined for some reason, because they don't know how to set goals for themselves or because they're setting the wrong goals."*

Tom helps his clients break out of their limiting beliefs then identify what really matters to them and how they can work to get it.

Don't settle.

Know where you are.

Know where you want to go.

Get moving.

Those ideas comprise Tom's philosophy in a nutshell.

CPSIA information can be obtained
at www.ICGtesting.com
Printed in the USA
FFOW03n0205080117
31116FF